OSHKOSH

NEW EDITION
OSHKOSH
THE WORLD'S BIGGEST AVIATION EVENT

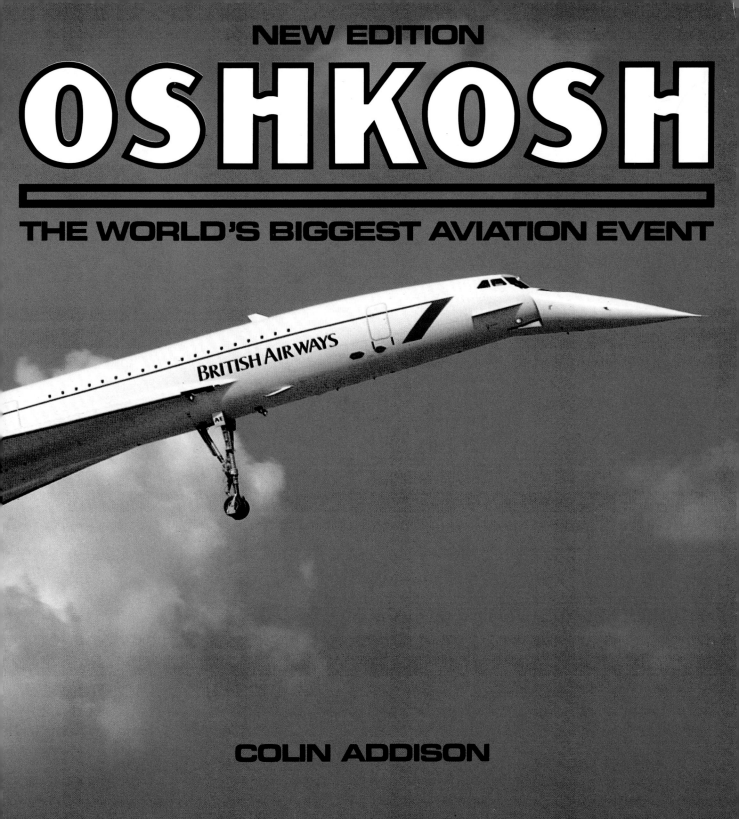

BRITISH AIRWAYS

COLIN ADDISON

For Tracey and James

Published in 1990 by Osprey Publishing Limited
59 Grosvenor Street, London W1X 9DA

British Library Cataloguing in Publication Data
Oshkosh, by gosh.
  1. United States. Displays
  I. Addison, Colin
  629.13′074′013

  ISBN 0-85045-972-9

Editor Dennis Baldry
Page design by David Tarbutt
Printed in Hong Kong

Front cover Now this is what
Oshkosh is all about; an amazing
assortment of beautifully restored
aircraft being enthused over by the
knowledgeable crowd at close
quarters. The Canadian Harvard Mk
IV in the foreground is absolutely
immaculate, but then so are the other
types in this panoramic view of the
Oshkosh flightline

Back cover Trailing smoke, a pair of
French-built Mudry CAP 10s zoom
over the crowd during the daily
flying display at Oshkosh. Over 230
CAP 10s have been built by Avions
Mudry

Right EAA Founder, Paul
Poberezny is one of the most
decorated men in the aviation
community, having received literally
hundreds of trophies and awards for
his contribution to sport aviation.
Even during his busy convention
schedule, Paul can be found finding
time to chat to his legions of disciples

Title pages Still the world's only
successful supersonic airliner,
Concorde serves the national carriers
of France and Britain. Two examples
of the seven strong British Airways
fleet have visited Oshkosh

Introduction

Lying on the shores of Lake Winnebago in the midwestern state of Wisconsin is the normally quiet, unassuming city of Oshkosh. Many of the locals work for the world-famous Oshkosh Truck Company or the equally well-known Oshkosh B'Gosh overalls manufacturer. For one week each year, however, the normally tranquil scene is transformed when 800,000 visitors descend on the area.

The reason for the sudden influx is quite simply that the most spectacular aviation event on the planet is underway. Known simply as 'Oshkosh', the Fly-in Convention is the annual international gathering of the Experimental Aircraft Association.

Wittman Regional Airport explodes in a scene of hectic activity with traffic ranging from ultralights to modern military hardware. Every inch of available space is used until the airport is swamped with up to 15,000 aeroplanes. Every single motel room, camping ground and university dormitory for over fifty miles is filled. The event has a greater crowd-pulling capability than even the Kentucky Derby, Rose Bowl or Indy 500. Aircraft movements during the week make Oshkosh busier than the world's busiest airport at Chicago O'Hare.

When the EAA was formed in 1953, its founder, Paul Poberezny, could not have imagined the status which his organization would hold today. From humble beginnings when Paul and a small group of friends held meetings in his basement at Hales Corner, the EAA now boasts a membership of 125,000. The organization was originally conceived to foster friendship amongst those like-minded people who wanted to design, build and fly their own aeroplanes.

Late in 1953 the EAA decided to sponsor their first fly-in. In September of that year a small number of aeroplanes flew in to Curtiss-Wright Field, Milwaukee. By the end of the 1950's enthusiasts flocked to Milwaukee in such numbers that the airfield could not longer handle the assembled masses. The 1960 fly-in saw a change of venue when the much more spacious airport at Rockford, Illinois was used.

The Rockford years saw continued growth in both the Fly-in and the amateur built aircraft movement. The scope of the event was broadened to include antiques and the blossoming warbird movement. The Fly-in by this time had become a Convention, and additional seminars, forums and workshops were scheduled.

The move to Oshkosh took place in 1970 and was a monumental undertaking. Between early spring and the opening day in late July a totally new convention site had been created.

EAA Oshkosh is now a mature event which is unsurpassed in the world of aviation. Renowned for organization, spotless grounds and activities, the show is now a model for fly-ins across the USA.

Disciples of the EAA travel from every state in the USA and most countries around the world. An instant town springs up within the convention site known as Camp Scholler, becoming temporary home for 40,000 visitors. Facilities range from a mini-mall, country market and restaurants to nightly entertainment and movies.

The immense scale, diversity and intoxicating atmosphere are a tribute to founder Paul Poberezny, his son Tom (Convention Chairman since 1977), and the army of volunteers who make the Convention simply the best.

Contents

EAA Air Adventure Museum

When the EAA Air Museum opened its doors in 1983 it was the culmination of a dream to open an aviation museum for the general public. What began as a few aeroplanes in modest surroundings has now grown into one of the most outstanding private aviation museums in the world. The impressive museum building is situated in beautifully landscaped surroundings close to Interstate 41 and just four blocks from the Wittman control tower. Adjoining the museum complex is Pioneer Airport which houses many of the EAA Foundation vintage aircraft. At weekends, weather permitting, some of these aircraft are flown.

The museum has been constructed on a lavish scale and at present houses nearly 80 of the 200 aircraft in the EAA inventory. The first impression on entering the museum is the professional standard by which the exhibits have been presented. Aircraft are expertly illuminated, often suspended from the ceiling, or mounted in groups detailing one particular aspect of aviation history.

The entrance hall features three Pitts Specials suspended in a dramatic bomb-burst arrangement. The museum complex has six galleries of flight featuring different aspects of EAA activity. Visitors are also able to see two theatre presentations and browse through galleries showing top quality aviation photographs and artwork.

One of the most expensive projects ever undertaken by the museum was the recent construction of the Eagle Hangar. This impressive building rekindles memories of those who fought and served in World War II. The hangar is not intended as a glorification of war but to remember those men, women and aircraft from the war years.

As the visitor enters the Eagle Hangar one of the most impressive sights is the 120-foot world mural which spans the entire width of the rear wall. The mural indicates the dispersal of aerial fighting units and the most significant aircraft used in the conflict. At the base of the mural are display cases which include historical information and memorabilia.

Amongst the aircraft displayed are the Foundation's Boeing B-17G Flying Fortress, XP-51 Mustang and P-38 Lightning. Other exhibits include news-reel footage describing both life on the frontline and everyday life back home during the turbulent years.

Any visit to the EAA Convention would be incomplete without a visit to the Air Adventure Museum.

This plinth mounted F-86 Sabre draws the attention of motorists on Interstate 41 to the Air Adventure Museum

General museum view showing some of the exhibits in the 'History of Flight' section, including a Curtiss EA-1, Monocoupe 113 and Fokker Dr.1

Top left The author's reflection caught in the polished spinner of a Beech Staggerwing in the EAA Air Adventure Museum

Left In 1931 Jimmy Doolittle won the Bendix Trophy race in the Laird 'Super Solution'. In 1980 members of the Florida Sport Aviation Antique & Classic Association completed the fine replica now displayed in the air racing section of the EAA museum complex

Right Amongst the aircraft exhibits representing the history of aerobatics are a 650 hp Super Stearman and the Super Chipmunk once owned by the late aerobatic genius Art Scholl

Left The EAA Aviation Foundation B-17G and F8F-2 Bearcat form part of the extensive warbird collection housed in the Eagle Hangar

Right Restoration of the Foundation's P-38L Lightning was completed in 1989. It has been painted in the colours of Wisconsin native Richard Bong's aircraft. Bong, America's 'Ace of Aces', scored 40 victories in the Pacific conflict. Also on show are examples of the J2F-6 Duck and Nakajima *Oscar*

In the absence of the real man, a cardboard replica will suffice! The life size Paul Poberezny cut-out stands beside a Lincoln PT-K welcoming visitors to Pioneer Airport

Pioneer Airport is home for Stinson
SM-1 Detroiter N1026

EAA Warbirds of America

During World War II the sky was literally filled with military aircraft representing the latest in technological aeronautical achievement of the era. After the war almost all of these machines were committed to the torch.

Now, only a very small percentage remain. The EAA Warbirds of America attempt to preserve these rare and beautiful aircraft which played such a vital role in fighting for democratic freedom.

Using the now well known motto 'Keep 'em Flying', members of the Warbirds of America perpetuate the memory of the fighting machines that served us all so well during World War II, restoring mighty bombers and fighters to their original magnificence. Today the movement incorporates post war military aircraft including small liaison types and trainers, all of which are lovingly maintained.

At each Oshkosh Convention the Warbirds of America thrill the crowds with their precision flying and highly polished formation routines. No other event offers the visitor the opportunity to view so many of these old aircraft in one place. It is not unusual to walk the warbird flightlines and count literally hundreds of these cherished aircraft.

Membership into the Warbirds of America is open to any one who is already a member of the EAA.

Early morning on the warbird ramp. The peace of the warbird park will be shattered when the Wright engines of these T-28 Trojans burst into life for another airshow spectacular

Left Derived from the Beech Bonanza, the Mentor tandem two-seat trainer first flew in 1948. The type was ordered into production for the USAF as the T-34A with 350 examples being produced by Beech and a further 100 by the Canadian Car Foundry. The US Navy procured 423 of the later T-34B variant. A fine

blue sky makes a complementary backdrop for these two immaculate examples of the T-34

Above A neat and seemingly endless line of T-34s taxi for take-off

Overleaf The T-34 has become very popular amongst the warbird fraternity. Excellent handling characteristics and performance contribute to their popularity. As many as 34 of the type have been seen flying *en masse* at the Convention

Right Any colour as long as it's yellow! A large percentage of the T-34 population wears this bright trainer livery

Below Three T-28As fly past in formation. Whilst two 'A' Models were evaluated by the US Navy in 1952 none served operationally

Non standard spinner, and a civilian
paint scheme set this T-28 apart from
the masses

Probably unique on the US warbird circuit is the Swiss-built Pilatus PC-7 N7TP, seen here escorting a pair of T-34s

Homeward bound, a T-28B departs a
crowded Convention scene for North
Carolina

Left Mother of five and grandmother of twelve, Sue Parish holds the distinction of being the first lady to serve as an EAA warbirds director. Sue has attended every convention since 1969 and can usually be seen flying her pink P-40N

Below A T-28A gets airborne from Wittman Regional Airport. TL-596 is one of 1194 'A' model Trojans built before production of the variant ceased in 1953. Several of this early model lingered on in Air National Guard service until 1959

Right A T-28B and T-28C hold tight formation during a 'Warbirds of America' display. The 'C' model is easily distinguished, being fitted with arrestor gear

AD-4 Skyraider N23827 regularly
travels the short distance from
Michigan to be part of the annual
Convention

Although designed as a shipboard interceptor, the F7F Tigercat was only issued to shore-based elements of the US Marine Corps, the first production aircraft appearing in 1944. After retiring from military service, several aircraft were converted for fire fighting duties, one example being NX700F which is now flown by John Ellis of the Kalamazoo Air Zoo

Of the 12,275 Hellcats built by
Grumman Aircraft of Bethpage, only
21 are known to survive. The Lone
Star Flight Museum completed
restoration of their two-seat F6F-5 in
time for the 1989 show season. The
aircraft is finished in the markings of
World War II ace, Alexander Vraciu

Bob Pond's Planes of Fame East
operate a host of old military
hardware. Amongst the many assets
is this F6F-5 Hellcat

Right Even on the ground the P-51 is a demanding aircraft. Due to the high nose profile forward vision is restricted. Here, Harry Tope cranes his neck in an attempt to catch a clear view of the flightline marshaller

Below The P-51 prototype flew for the first time on the 26th October 1940. Designer Edgar Schmued could hardly have envisaged that some fifty years afterwards large numbers of these potent machines would be flying in the hands of private individuals. Harry Tope owns this chequer-tailed P-51D NL51HT

Left Canadian Gary McCann is one of the few who prefers to operate his P-51D in civilian guise. The immaculate gloss-black aircraft registered C-FFUZ is a Convention regular

Below Several training programmes exist to aid the 'would-be' P-51 pilot. Dr Joseph Scogna of Yardley, Pennsylvania offers type conversion on his rare TP-51D *Baby Duck*

Far Left Hess Bomberger is an avid supporter of EAA events in his P-51D *Vergeltungswaffe*

Left 'Yosemite Sam' forms part of the artwork on P-51D *Six Shooter*

Below Tom Wood of Indianapolis owns bright green P-51D NL6306T

Only two airworthy examples of the famous British Avro Lancaster bomber survive today. The Canadian Warplane Heritage aircraft was a debutant at Oshkosh '89

Right The proud crew of Lancaster C-GVRA prepare for take-off

The Planes of Fame East F4U Corsair
starts up under the watchful eye of
flightline safety personnel

BT-13 *Silver Thunder* is one of only a
few survivors from the 7832 Valiants
built by the Vultee Aircraft Company

The North American T-6 celebrated
its fiftieth birthday in 1988. Known
affectionately as the 'Pilotmaker', the
type has moulded the careers of
many military aviators. Eighty-two
T-6s registered at Oshkosh '88
including N3717G *Prime Time*

Bill Leff has become a popular
airshow act in his modified and
highly polished T-6

Flying the flag, North American
AT-6 N1364N is owned by Warbird
Leasing of Maryland

Overleaf A neat double line-up
comprising mainly of T-6s with a
lone North American Yale interloper

Below North American SNJ-5
N15HB tucks away its undercarriage

These pages and overleaf A long-time tradition in military aviation has been the application of colourful artwork by air crews to their aircraft. Today many warbird owners keep up the tradition, though often with spurious markings. *Spanish Lady, Chuck Wagon, Slow-Mo-Shun, Brer Rabbit* and *Snoopy* are worn by a variety of T-6s

The EAA Aviation Foundation keeps B-25 Mitchell N10V *City of Burlington* in flying order

Right Artwork on *City of Burlington*

Below Paul Poberezny completes a smooth roller landing in the B-25

Kermit Weeks operates his
de Havilland Mosquito from his
facility at Tamiami Airport, Florida.
The aircraft is one of only two
airworthy examples

Overleaf A large number of
civilian-built Cessna 337 Super
Skymasters are now flying in pseudo
military marks masquerading as the
military O-2 derivative

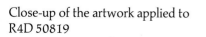

Close-up of the artwork applied to
R4D 50819

Hughes OH-6A *Miss Clawd IV* is one
of a large number to have served
with the United States Army. The
helicopter was originally conceived
from the civilian model 500. This
example is now on the airshow
circuit

Eighteen Bell 47K helicopters were
sold to the US Navy for instrument
training and designated TH-13Ns.
This example built in 1957 has
recently been restored

Classic Jets

Undoubtedly the fastest growing aspect of the warbird movement is the number of ex-military jets operating in civilian hands. The piston warbird operators have been quick to accept this new development and both categories can be seen operating side-by-side from the Oshkosh warbird area.

The upturn in activity, particularly in the last couple of years, is due to the disposal of earlier-generation jet equipment. Amongst the first types passing into civilian ownership were small numbers of Vampires, T-33s and North American F-86s.

The USA is the hub of warbird jet operations with several commercial enterprises specializing in military jet restoration work. Some indication of the size of the movement is the fact that by early 1989 around 200 of these obsolete machines graced the US civil register. Although many of that number are T-33s there are also large numbers of Fouga Magisters and Hispano HA-200s from Europe, and now even dozens of MiG variants.

1989 saw the formation of the Classic Jet Aircraft Association to foster better

Left and right hand views of the Combat Jets Flying Museum Canadair Sabre *The Huff*. The markings are a fine representation of those worn by an F-86 in Korea

understanding between jet warbird owners and the FAA, and to promote safe and sensible operation of these demanding aircraft.

Within the next few years it is not inconceivable that early F-4 Phantom IIs or similarly more advanced military jets will be gracing the EAA Convention in civilian ownership.

John Dilley gets airborne in his
F-86A Sabre N178/FU-178

Once familiar to European
enthusiasts when registered
G-HUNT, this bright red Hunter F.51
is now based in Texas with the
Combat Jets Flying Museum

Designed and built under the supervision of Professor Messerschmitt, the Hispano Saeta (Arrow) tandem two-seat trainer served with the Spanish Air Force as the E.14. Today large numbers of the type are in the hands of warbird aviators

Ex-Chinese Navy Shenyang J-4 (a
license-built Mikoyan MiG-15)
N15MG rolling for take-off

Restoration work on A-4C Skyhawk
N3E was completed in 1989. The
aircraft now forms part of the
Combat Jets Flying Museum

From Jennies to Jets

Being the world's largest aviation event, it is hardly surprising that the afternoon air shows at Oshkosh are spectacular.

Where else in the world would it be possible to see everything from a Curtiss Jenny through military fast jets and warbirds to wide-bodied jetliners?

Since the main north-south runway at Wittman Regional Airport was extended it has become possible for almost any existing type of aircraft to visit the Convention. During the same development programme the opportunity was taken to create new hardstanding areas for the heavyweight static exhibits.

In 1988 a British Airways Concorde supersonic airliner shared top honours with a Rockwell B-1B bomber. Whilst Concorde had visited Oshkosh on an earlier occasion, the additional runway length added a much greater safety margin.

Unbelievably, 1989 topped the previous year with the appearance of the mighty Russian Antonov An-124 transport, the SR-71 Blackbird and 233 qualified pilots ensconced in a Qantas Boeing 747.

Famous names from the world of aerobatics and stunt flying are always in evidence, such as Bob Hoover, Bob Herendeen and the French Connection to name but three. These people return annually to volunteer their services free of charge to provide breathtaking displays for the amassed crowd.

Below TAV-8B of the US Marine Corps' VMAT-203, based at MCAS Cherry Point in North Carolina

Red Baron Frozen Pizza sponsors this four-ship Stearman team

Boeing KC-135R crosses the threshold

Below The mighty Rockwell B-1B was a prestigious attraction at the 1988 Convention

Overleaf Photographed from the roof of the FAA pavilion, this view shows a small section of the homebuilt park, with the EAA B-17 *Aluminium Overcast* dominating the foreground

The spirit of *glasnost* arrived at Oshkosh '89 in the shape of the huge Antonov An-124 transport. The crew became local celebrities and were often seen signing autographs for the assembled crowds. They won a place in the hearts of many Convention visitors when they were seen waving the US flag from their flight deck during their display routine

Left The An-124 has a crew of six, a wing span of 240 feet and a length of 228 feet

Below left The four Lotarev D-18T turbofans propel the An-124 into an impressive climb after take-off

Below A crew member of the An-124 waves the US flag

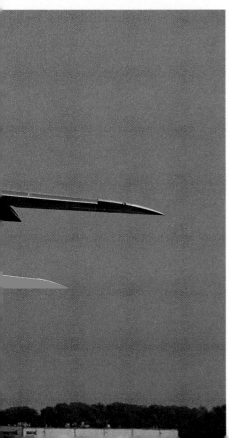

Six Curtiss JN-4 Jennies gathered at
Oshkosh '89 out of a possible total of
twelve remaining airworthy.
Amongst those attending was the
mount of Wally Olsen built in 1917

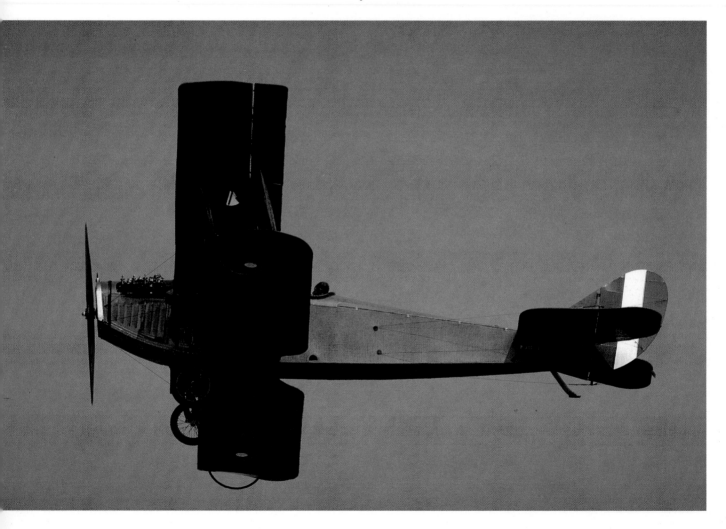

Speedbird Alpha Alpha is guided by a marshaller into its designated parking spot

The scope of the Convention is evident in this view showing a Rutan Long-Eze and Concorde

Right Extra 300 N89BR is the mount of US aerobatic champion Clint McHenry

Below Warren Basler's FBO facility at Wittman Field provides both refuelling and maintenance during Convention week. However the bulk of Basler's work centres around restoration and refurbishment of DC-3s. To date some 80 of these venerable old workhorses have passed through the workshops on the north side of the airport. The company operate 14 of them on freight duties on behalf of such companies as Federal Express, UPS and Emery. Among the fleet is a turboprop conversion

Below Qantas Boeing 747 *Oshkosh Express* making a low flypast at the 1989 Convention. This aircraft flew into the record books when it alighted at Oshkosh with 233 qualified pilots on board

Right Throttles open, the four Rolls-Royce RB.211 engines spool up for a dusty take-off

Antiques/Classics

In the early days of aviation, pilots donned leather jackets and goggles and more often than not tossed a white scarf over their shoulder. This is the romantic image often associated with the sight of an old biplane. Whilst aviation has progressed beyond recognition from those glorious early days, there are those who still delight in the notions of yesteryear.

The EAA Antiques & Classics division has a membership dedicated to the era when man strove to fly higher, faster, further. Those early pioneers were the foundation of today's sport aviation movement.

Each year at the Oshkosh convention it is possible to walk from the famous 'Red Barn' (the Antiques/Classic headquarters building) and travel back in time to the formative years. Row after row of aircraft, Staggerwings, Cubs, Stearmans and Wacos are some of those available for inspection. The craftsmanship and skill of the original manufacturer and the restorer are clearly visible. It is possible to trace the advancement from the earliest cloth covered wing to the later fabric and tube creations which materialized in the 1950s.

The EAA defines an antique aeroplane as one constructed by the original manufacturer (or licensee) on or before the last day of 1945. Aircraft constructed between 1945 and 1955 are defined as classics.

Although some of the antiques and classics have remained airworthy throughout their existence, many have not. Quite a few of the championship-winning examples presented at Oshkosh over the years have been almost completely new airframes, with a high percentage of newly manufactured parts, built from scratch. It is hard to imagine a dust-covered skeleton, possibly found in a barn, breathing new life maybe half a century after original construction.

An indication of the size and scope of the antique/classic movement is the fact that almost fifty percent of showplanes registered at Oshkosh are from this category. In addition to seeing these aircraft on the flightline some of them take to the air in the annual 'Parade of Flight'.

The Phantom side-by-side two-seat monoplane first appeared in 1934, and was the first product of the Luscombe Airplane Corporation. The Phantom was advanced for its time, featuring a stressed-skin duralumin monocoque fuselage. This is the sole airworthy example of 25 built

Below First flown in 1939, the Cessna T-50 Bobcat served in both civil and military guises. At the 1989 Convention, no fewer than eight examples gathered at Wittman Field for a reunion organised by Dick Hill. Amongst their number was *Bimbo Bomber* shown on start-up

Right The Stinson SM-6000B tri-motor first appeared in 1930. The type gained high acclaim, being less than half the price of other tri-motor equipment of the period. Many Convention visitors have had the privilege of a pleasure flight in this magnificent black aircraft

Below right Distinguished by the negative stagger of its wings, the Beech 17 Staggerwing first appeared in 1932. Many examples of the various marks of Staggerwing are still airworthy today

Many highly colourful examples of
the Boeing Stearman can be viewed
in the antiques/classics parking area

The DGA-15 five-seat cabin monoplane was introduced by the Howard Aircraft Company in 1939. Fred Kirk, of Fort Lauderdale, Florida owns bright red example NC22423

Production of the Cessna 195 began in 1947 and continued until 1954 when 955 examples had left the factory. The finish on N3491V is probably better than when it was originally delivered

In 1942 Piper Aircraft were contracted to modify their J-5C for the hospital evacuation role. Becoming the HE-1, the aircraft was able to carry the pilot and one stretcher-bound passenger. Ken Hughes and Ray Mull of EAA Chapter 585 restored this example in Michigan

Originally conceived in 1927, this
Monocoupe is owned by the EAA
Aviation Foundation

The Taylorcraft Aviation Company
was formed in 1936 and produced
several fine high-wing cabin
monoplane types. The company was
the predecessor of the Piper Aircraft
Corporation

Right In recent years the basic Chipmunk airframe has provided the basis for many conversions to Super Chipmunk status. This bright yellow example is fitted with a 260 bhp Lycoming engine and enlarged fin and rudder

Below right Designed by de Havilland Canada, the Chipmunk two-seat primary trainer first flew in May 1946. It was subsequently produced in both Canada and Britain. Some Canadian examples have a clear-view blown canopy such as on the bare metal example shown here

Below This Waco cabin biplane is a regular visitor to Oshkosh

The Bücker Bü 131 Jungmann was produced in large numbers in Germany and under licence in Spain and Czechoslavakia. Dating back to 1934, the type can still be found in quantity around Europe and several have been imported into North America

The three Waco UPF.7s in this view
were all the product of one
restoration workshop in Indiana

Left During 1977 the EAA Aviation Foundation re-enacted the tour of North America made by Lindbergh after his epic journey to Paris. The Ryan NYP replica *Spirit of St Louis* was escorted by the Foundation owned Stinson SM-8 Junior NC408Y

Below Built in 1929, Travel Air D-4000 NC671H is powered by a 220 hp Continental engine, instead of the original Wright J-6

Below left Twenty Pheasant H-10s were originally produced, and only one airworthy example survives today. The aircraft, powered by a Curtiss OX-5 engine was restored by its EAA owners

The Lighter Side

The EAA was originally founded to foster interest, understanding and friendship amongst those wishing to build their own aircraft. It is therefore hardly surprising that the movement owes so much to those who conceived the association almost 40 years ago.

In those early days, homebuilt aircraft weren't particularly attractive and, in the eyes of many, left much to be desired. Homebuilders were sometimes even considered strange by those with little imagination or outlook. However, for those individuals who had spent many hours working materials into their very own flying machine the gratification was overwhelming.

Walking around the homebuilts park at Oshkosh today, it is easy to see the advancement in do-it-yourself technology. One man above all others has given the homebuilt movement the boost and respect which it so rightly deserves. That man is Burt Rutan, who designed the Vari-Eze, Long-Eze, Quickie and Vari-Viggen. Most of these designs rely almost totally on composite materials and today the homebuilt park is almost exclusively a sea of glass.

The stability of today's designs has resulted in a far better understanding throughout the aviation world. Indeed, ideas conceived for the homebuilder have had a great impact on products from some of the commercial aircraft manufacturers.

It is now possible to build your own aircraft with outstanding performance, range and comfort. High performance designs such as the Swearingen SX-300, Glasair and Cirrus can be highly labour-intensive, but the resulting product will be one of great personal pride.

In a different perspective of light aviation, but with a similar desire in mind, there are the ultralights. These generally brightly coloured aircraft are the least restricted method of flying and therefore create a sense of freedom for those who have neither the means nor the desire to go through the rigorous tests required for other types of aviation.

Ultralights have evolved from merely a powered hang glider to today's more conventional aeroplane styles. Even so, the only limits to them are a maximum cruise speed of 55 mph and stall speed of 26 mph, a weight of no more than 254 pounds and they can carry as little as five gallons of fuel. A small price to pay for freedom.

View of the homebuilt headquarters building and parking area

Overleaf Looking north across the homebuilt area to the warbird park

Left The colourful artwork on Silhouette N88KG does much to enhance the pleasing lines of this homebuilt project

Below left In keeping with its namesake the Lake Buccaneer, the Buccaneer ultralight is also an amphibious design

Below Rotorway have designed a number of homebuilt helicopters including the very popular Executive

Overleaf The tandem two-seat Air & Space 18 was designed by Raymond Umbaugh and was flown as long ago as 1959. The three-blade rotor is powered for take-off by a clutch between the engine transmission and rotor shaft, this design giving the machine the ability to 'jump' start

A trio of Rand KR-2 homebuilts

The Taylor Monoplane has for many
years been one of the most popular
designs for the homebuilder

At the top end of the homebuilt market is the highly sophisticated composite Cirrus, a luxurious four-place pusher

Immaculate example of the Midget
Mustang

Below The Replica Fighter Association have their own designated parking area at Oshkosh. Amongst those attending a recent Convention was this S.E.5a replica

Right N4622X is a very accurate scale representation of the Japanese *Zero*

Below right An early attempt at scale warbird representation was this T-6 look-alike N794E. Parts were used from several production types including the undercarriage assembly from a Cessna 195

Wet
Wet
Wet

Running simultaneously with the annual EAA Convention at Oshkosh is the 'Splash-in' which takes place at the Brennan Seaplace Base on the shores of Lake Winnebago, many of the visitors to this event being members of both the EAA and Seaplane Pilots' Association.

Away from the hustle and bustle of Wittman Regional Airport the seaplane base offers refuge for dozens of amphibians. Here, floatplanes ranging from Piper Cubs to the larger Grumman species come and go from the idyllic cove setting.

Many of the visitors to the seaplane base arrive from Canada where floatplane flying can be a necessary part of their everyday travel.

Others may have taken up this form of flying purely for recreational purposes and to enjoy flying with an added dimension.

So there they sit, resplendent in their rural surroundings, probably the most peaceful, yet often overlooked part of the Oshkosh event.

Connie Edwards intends to fly his HU-16E Albatros around the world to celebrate 200 years of the US Coast Guard

Left A temperamental Wright R-1820 engine caused problems for the crew of this ex-Chilean Navy HU-16 at a recent convention

Below left Dennis Buehn restored his HU-16 from a decaying hulk found at the MASDC facility at Davis-Monthan, Arizona

Below Grumman Widgeon receiving close scrutiny from a pair of bathers

Overleaf General view across Brennan Seaplane Base with an assortment of Cessnas and a J-3 Cub

Left Aircraft are tied by their propellors to anchorage points on the lake bed, giving them freedom to turn into the prevailing wind

Below left Piper Super Cubs make delightful amphibians

Below After a busy day's flying, the owner drops the anchor from his Aeronca

Aircraft visiting the seaplane base are
usually moored away from the
registration and refuelling area.
A small fleet of boats are provided as
aircraft tugs

A rare Howard DGA-15 floatplane shown sharing the lake with a water skier

Overleaf J-3 Cub about to depart on a local sortie around Lake Winnebago